THIS BOOK

BELONGS TO. . .

_____

_____

# The Beloved Poetry of
# HELEN STEINER RICE

BARBOUR
PUBLISHING

ISBN 978-1-59789-965-9

The poetry of Helen Steiner Rice is published under a licensing agreement with the Helen Steiner Rice Foundation.

Special thanks to Virginia J. Ruehlmann for her cooperation and assistance in the development of this book.

Published by Barbour Publishing, Inc., P.O. Box 719, Uhrichsville, Ohio 44683, www.barbourbooks.com

*Our mission is to publish and distribute inspirational products offering exceptional value and biblical encouragement to the masses.*

Member of the
Evangelical Christian
Publishers Association

Printed in Malaysia.

Here in one volume, *The Beloved Poetry of Helen Steiner Rice* features a special selection of poetry penned by America's best-loved poet. Her inspirational verse, as well as an index, allows you to find poems relating to specific topics such as God's love, comfort, praise, and prayer.

Born in Ohio in 1900, Helen Steiner Rice began writing at an early age. In 1918, Helen took a job at a public utilities company, eventually becoming one of the first female advertising managers and public speakers in the country. At age 29, she married banker Franklin Rice, who committed suicide in 1932, never having recovered mentally and financially from losses incurred during the Great Depression.

Following her husband's death, Helen used her gift of verse to encourage others. Her talents came to the attention of the nation when her greeting card poem "The Priceless Gift of Christmas" was read on the Lawrence Welk Show. Soon a series of poetry books, a source of inspiration to people worldwide, followed. Helen died in 1981, leaving a foundation that offers assistance to the needy and elderly.

May Helen Steiner Rice's powerful words encourage, strengthen, and renew your spirit, leaving you filled with God's peace, love, joy, and hope.

*Thank* You, God, for the beauty
around me everywhere,
The gentle rain and glistening dew,
the sunshine and the air,
The joyous gift of feeling the soul's soft,
whispering voice
That speaks to me from deep within
and makes my heart rejoice.

*God* has told us that nothing can sever

A life He created to live forever.

So let God's promise soften our sorrow

And give us new strength for a brighter tomorrow.

*Our* Father in heaven, whose love is divine,

Thanks for the love of a mother like mine.

In Thy great mercy look down from above

And grant this dear mother the gift of Your love.

*Birthdays* are the gateway to

An endless life of joy for you

If you but pray from day to day

That He will show you the truth and the way.

*While* we can't see what's on death's other side,

We know that our Father will richly provide

All that He promised to those who believe,

And His kingdom is waiting for us to receive.

*Into* His hands each night as I sleep

I commend my soul for the dear Lord to keep,

Knowing that if my soul should take flight

It will soar to the land where there is no night.

*God* asks for no credentials—

   He accepts us with our flaws.

He is kind and understanding

   and He welcomes us because

We are His erring children and He loves us, every one,

And He freely and completely

   forgives all that we have done,

Asking only if we're ready

   to follow where He leads,

Content that in His wisdom

   He will answer all our needs.

*Life's* a mystery man can't understand,

The great giver of life is holding our hands,

And safe in His care there is no need for seeing,

"For in Him we live and move and have our being."

*We* have God's Easter promise, so let us seek a goal

That opens up new vistas for man's eternal soul. . .

For our strength and our security

    lie not in earthly things

But in Christ the Lord, who died for us

    and rose as King of kings.

*When* your nervous network
becomes a tangled mess,
Just close your eyes in silent prayer
and ask the Lord to bless
Each thought that you are thinking,
each decision you must make,
As well as every word you speak
and every step you take.

*A man* may be wealthy,

Good fortune may be his fate,

But only man's motives

Can make him truly great.

*We* know we are born to die and arise,

For beyond this world in beauty lies

The purpose of living and the ultimate goal

God gives at birth to each seeking soul.

*Trust* God's all wise wisdom

And doubt the Father never,

For in His heavenly kingdom

There is nothing lost forever.

*I said* a special prayer for you—
I asked the Lord above
To keep you safely in His care
and enfold you in His love.
I did not ask for fortune,
for riches, or for fame,
I only asked for blessings
in the Holy Savior's name—
Blessings to surround you
in times of trial and stress,
And inner joy to fill your heart
with peace and happiness.

*May* peace and understanding

Give you strength and courage, too,

And may the hours and days ahead

Hold a new hope for you;

For the sorrow that is yours today

Will pass away and then

You'll find the sun of happiness

Will shine for you again.

If I walked not with sorrow and lived not with loss,

Would my soul seek sweet solace

at the foot of the cross?

If all I desired was mine day by day,

Would I kneel before God and earnestly pray?

I ask myself this and the answer is plain—

If my life were all pleasure and I never knew pain,

I'd seek God less often and need Him much less,

For God's sought more often in times of distress—

And no one knows God or sees Him as plain

As those who have met Him

    on the pathway of pain.

*Life* can't always be a song—

You have to have trouble to make you strong,

So whenever you are troubled

  and everything goes wrong,

It is just God working in you

  to make your spirit strong.

*Often* during a busy day

I pause for a minute to silently pray,

I mention the names of those I love

And treasured friends I am fondest of—

For it doesn't matter where we pray

If we honestly mean the words we say,

For God is always listening to hear

The prayers that are made by a heart that's sincere.

*Our* Father tells His children
   that if they would know His will
They must seek Him in the silence
   when all is calm and still. . .
For nature's great forces
   are found in quiet things
Like softly falling snowflakes
   drifting down on angels' wings.

*God,* give us wider vision
        to see and understand
That both the sunshine and the showers
        are gifts from Thy great hand,
And then at last may we accept
        the sunshine and the shower,
Confident it takes them both
        to make salvation ours.

*There* is nothing that is new

     beneath God's timeless sun,

And present, past, and future

     are all molded into one.

For the restless, unknown longing

     of my searching soul won't cease

Until God comes in glory

     and my soul at last finds peace.

*Friendship* is a priceless gift
that can't be bought or sold,
And to have an understanding friend
is worth far more than gold. . .
And the golden chain of friendship
is a strong and blessed tie
Binding kindred hearts together
as the years go passing by.

*God* sends to the heart

  in its winter of sadness

A springtime awakening

  of new hope and gladness,

And loved ones who sleep

  in a season of death

Will, too, be awakened

  by God's life-giving breath.

*With* God on your side, it matters not who

Is working to keep life's good things from you,

For you need nothing more

　　than God's guidance and love

To ensure you the things

　　that you're most worthy of.

*Framed* by the vast, unlimited sky,

Bordered by mighty waters,

Sheltered by beautiful woodland groves,

Scented with flowers that bloom and die,

Protected by giant mountain peaks

The land of the great unknown

Snowcapped and towering, a nameless place

That beckons man on as the gold he seeks,

Bubbling with life and earthly joys

Reeking with pain and mortal strife

Dotted with wealth and material gains

Built on ideals of girls and boys,

Streaked with toil, opportunity's banner unfurled

Stands out the masterpiece of art

Painted by the one great God

A picture of the world.

*You* are ushering in another day,

    untouched and freshly new,

So here I am to ask You, God, if You'll renew me, too. . .

Forgive the many errors that I made yesterday

And let me try again, dear God,

    to walk closer in Thy way. . .

But, Father, I am well aware I can't make it on my own,

So take my hand and hold it tight for I can't walk alone.

34

*Death* is just a natural thing,

   like the closing of a door

As we start up on a journey to a new and distant shore. . .

And none need make this journey undirected or alone,

For God promised us safe passage

   to this vast and great unknown.

*Give* Him a chance to open His treasures,

And He'll fill your life with unfathomable pleasures—

Pleasures that never grow worn out and faded

And leave us depleted, disillusioned, and jaded—

For God has a storehouse just filled to the brim

With all that man needs, if we'll only ask Him.

*Where* there is love the heart is light,

Where there is love the day is bright.

Where there is love there is a song

To help when things are going wrong.

*You* ask me how I know it's true

that there is a living God.

A God who rules the universe—

the sky, the sea, the sod—

A God who holds all creatures

in the hollow of His hand,

A God who put infinity

in one tiny grain of sand,

A God who made the seasons—

winter, summer, fall, and spring—

And put His flawless rhythm

into each created thing,

A God who hangs the sun out slowly
    with the break of day
And gently takes the stars in and puts the night away,
A God whose mighty handiwork defies the skill of man,
For no architect can alter God's perfect master plan.
What better answers are there
    to prove His holy being
Than the wonders all around us
    that are ours just for the seeing.

*Blessed* are the people who learn to accept

The trouble men try to escape and reject,

For in accordance we're given great grace

And courage and faith and strength to face

The daily troubles that come to us all,

So we may learn to stand straight and tall. . .

For the grandeur of life is born of defeat,

For in overcoming we make life complete.

*With* faith in your heart, reach out for God's hand
And accept what He sends,
  though you can't understand. . .
For our Father in heaven always knows
  what is best,
And if you trust His wisdom,
  your life will be blessed.

*April* comes with cheeks a-glowing

Silver streams are all a-flowing,

Flowers open wide their eyes

In lovely rapturous surprise.

Lilies dream beside the brooks,

Violets in meadow nooks,

And the birds gone wild with glee

Fill the woods with melody.

*There* are always two sides—the good and the bad,

The dark and the light, the sad and the glad...

But in looking back over the good and the bad,

We're aware of the number of good things we've had—

And in counting our blessings,

    we find when we're through

We've no reason at all to complain or be blue.

*Flowers* sleeping 'neath the snow,

Awakening when the spring winds blow,

Leafless trees so bare before

Gowned in lacy green once more,

Hard, unyielding, frozen sod

Now softly carpeted by God,

Still streams melting in the spring

Rippling over rocks that sing,

Barren, windswept, lonely hills

Turning gold with daffodils—

These miracles are all around

Within our sight and touch and sound,

As true and wonderful today

As when the stone was rolled away,

Proclaiming to all doubting men

That in God all things live again.

*There* is no garden so complete

But roses could make

   the place more sweet.

There is no life so rich and rare

But one more friend could enter there.

Like roses in a garden

   kindness fills the air

With bit of a certain sweetness

   as it touches everywhere.

*The* unexpected kindness

from an unexpected place,

A hand outstretched in friendship,

a smile on someone's face,

A word of understanding

spoken in a time of trial

Are unexpected miracles

that make life more worthwhile.

If we could just lift up our hearts

Like flowers to the sun

And trust His Easter promise

And pray, "Thy will be done,"

We'd find the peace we're seeking,

The kind no man can give—

The peace that comes from knowing

He died so we might live!

*All* of His treasures are yours to share

If you love Him completely

and show that you care. . .

And if you walk in His footsteps

and have faith to believe,

There's nothing you ask for

that you will not receive!

*Hear* me, blessed Jesus,

as I say my prayers today

And tell me You are close to me

and You'll never go away. . .

And tell me that You love me

like the Bible says You do,

And tell me also, Jesus,

I can always come to You.

*So* many things in the line of duty

Drain us of effort and leave us no beauty,

And the dust of the soul grows thick and unswept,

The spirit is drenched in tears unwept.

But just as we fall beside the road,

Discouraged with life and bowed down with our load,

We lift our eyes, and what seemed a dead end

Is the street of dreams where we meet a friend.

*Friendship* is a priceless gift
     that cannot be bought or sold
But its value is far greater
     than a mountain made of gold—
For gold is cold and lifeless, it can neither see nor hear,
And in the time of trouble it is powerless to cheer.

It has no ears to listen, no heart to understand,

It cannot bring you comfort

or reach out a helping hand—

So when you ask God for a gift be thankful if He sends

Not diamonds, pearls, or riches,

but the love of real true friends.

*Growing* older only means

The spirit grows serene

And we behold things with our souls

That our eyes have never seen.

For each birthday is a gateway

That leads to a reward,

The rich reward of learning,

The true greatness of the Lord.

*Friendship* is a golden chain,

the links are friends so dear,

And like a rare and precious jewel,

it's treasured more each year.

It's clasped together firmly with a love

that's deep and true,

And it's rich with happy memories

and fond recollections, too.

*Oh*, heavenly Father, grant again
A simple, childlike faith to men,
Forgetting color, race, and creed
And seeing only the heart's deep need.
For faith alone can save man's soul
And lead him to a higher goal.

*Love* alone can make us kind

And give us joy and peace of mind,

So live with joy unselfishly

And you'll be blessed abundantly.

*The* sleeping earth awakens,

 the robins start to sing—

The flowers open wide their eyes

 to tell us it is spring.

The bleakness of the winter

 is melted by the sun—

The tree that looked so stark and dead

 becomes a living one.

These miracles of Easter,

 wrought with divine perfection,

Are the blessed reassurance

 of our Savior's resurrection.

*With* faith, let go and let God lead the way

Into a brighter and less-troubled day.

For God has a plan for everyone,

If we learn to pray, "Thy will be done."

For nothing in life is without God's design

For each life is fashioned by the hand that's divine.

*Love* can transform the most commonplace

Into beauty and splendor and sweetness and grace.

Love is unselfish, understanding, and kind,

For it sees with its heart and not with its mind.

*Death* is a season that man must pass through,

And just like the flowers, God wakens him, too,

So why should we grieve when our loved ones die,

For we'll meet them again in a cloudless sky.

For Easter is more than a beautiful story—

It's the promise of life and eternal glory.

*God* has given us the answers,

which too often go unheeded,

But if we search His promises

we'll find everything that's needed

To lift our faltering spirits

and renew our courage, too,

For there's absolutely nothing

too much for God to do.

*Faith* to believe when the way is rough

And faith to hang on when the going is tough

Will never fail to pull us through

And bring us strength and comfort, too.

*We* rob our own lives much more than we know

When we fail to respond or in any way show

Our thanks for the blessings that daily are ours—

The warmth of the sun, the fragrance of flowers,

The beauty of twilight, the freshness of dawn,

The coolness of dew on a green velvet lawn,

For the joy of enjoying and the fullness of living

Are found in the heart that is filled with thanksgiving.

*Every* day is a reason for giving
And giving is the key to living. . .
So let us give ourselves away,
Not just today but every day.

*God* only asks us to do our best—

Then He will take over and finish the rest. . .

So when you are tired, discouraged, and blue,

There's always one door that is opened to you

And that is the door to the house of prayer,

And you'll find God waiting to meet you there.

*When* life becomes a problem

much too great for us to bear,

Instead of trying to escape,

let us withdraw in prayer—

For withdrawal means renewal

if we withdraw to pray

And listen in the quietness

to hear what God will say.

*Each* day at dawning I lift my heart high

And raise up my eyes to the infinite sky.

I watch the night vanish as a new day is born,

And I hear the birds sing on the wings of the morn.

I see the dew glisten in crystal-like splendor

While God, with a touch that is gentle and tender,

Wraps up the night and softly tucks it away

And hangs out the sun to herald a new day. . .

And so I give thanks and my heart kneels to pray,

"God, keep me and guide me and go with me today."

*A little* laughter, a little song,

A little teardrop

When things go wrong,

A little calm

And a little strife

A little loving—

And that is life.

*Give* me perception to make me aware

That scattered profusely on life's thoroughfare

Are the best gifts of God that we daily pass by

As we look at the world

with an unseeing eye.

*Praise* God for trouble that cuts like a knife

And disappointments that shatter your life,

For God is but testing your faith and your love

Before He appoints you to rise far above

All the small things that so sorely distress you,

For God's only intention

    is to strengthen and bless you.

*Father,* I have knowledge, so will You show me now

How to use it wisely and to find a way somehow

To make the world I live in a little better place

And to make life with its problems a bit easier to face?

Grant me faith and courage,

    and put purpose in my days,

And show me how to serve Thee

    in the most effective ways.

I'd like to be a raindrop

Just falling on your hand,

I'd like to be a blade of grass

On which your dear feet stand,

I'd like to be your shadow

As it moves around all day,

I'd like to be most anything

That hangs around your way.

*God's* love is like a beacon

burning bright with faith and prayer,

And through all the changing scenes of life

we can find a haven there.

*Thank* You, God, for little things

    that come unexpectedly

To brighten up a dreary day that dawned so dismally.

Thank You, God, for sending a happy thought my way

To blot out my depression on a disappointing day.

Thank You, God, for brushing the dark clouds

    from my mind

And leaving only sunshine and joy of heart behind.

*Hurrying* along life's thoroughfare,

We passed Him by but remained unaware

That within the very sight of our eyes,

Unnoticed, the Son of God passed by.

*Apple* blossoms bursting wide

    now beautify a tree

And make a springtime picture

    that is beautiful to see.

Oh fragrant, lovely blossoms,

    you'll make a bright bouquet

If I but break your branches

    from the apple tree today,

But if I but break your branches

    and make your beauty mine,

You'll bear no fruit in season

    when severed from the vine,

And when we cut ourselves away
    from guidance that's divine,
Our lives will be as fruitless
    as the branch without the vine.
For as the flowering branches
    depend upon the tree
To nourish and fulfill them
    till they reach futurity,
We, too, must be dependent
    on our Father up above,
For we are but the branches,
    and He's the tree of love.

*When* one sheds a teardrop or suffers loss in vain,

God is always there to turn our losses into gain. . .

And every burden born today and every present sorrow

Are but God's happy harbingers

    of a joyous, bright tomorrow.

*Life* is a sojourn here on earth

Which begins the day God gives us birth.

We enter this world from the great unknown,

And God gives each spirit

   a form of its own.

*God* did not promise sun without rain,

Light without darkness or joy without pain.

He only promised strength for the day

When the darkness comes and we lose our way.

*The* Lord is our salvation

and our strength in every fight,

Our redeemer and protector,

our eternal guiding light.

He has promised to sustain us,

He's our refuge from all harms,

And underneath this refuge

are the everlasting arms.

*At* this time may God grant you

Special gifts of joy and cheer,

And bless you for the good you do

For others through the year. . .

May you find rich satisfaction

In your daily work and prayer,

And in knowing as you serve Him

He will keep you in His care.

*The* rainbow is God's promise

of hope for you and me,

And though the clouds hang heavy

and the sun we cannot see,

We know above the dark clouds

that fill the stormy sky

Hope's rainbow will come shining through

when the clouds have drifted by.

*Everywhere* across the land

You see God's face and touch His hand

Each time you look up in the sky

Or watch the fluffy clouds drift by,

Or feel the sunshine, warm and bright,

Or watch the dark night turn to light,

Or hear a bluebird brightly sing,

Or see the winter turn to spring,

Or stop to pick a daffodil,

Or gather violets on some hill,

Or touch a leaf or see a tree,

It's all God whispering, "This is Me. . .

And I am faith and I am light

And in Me there shall be no night."

*Meet* Him in the morning

and go with Him through the day

And thank Him for His guidance

each evening when you pray—

And if you follow faithfully

this daily way to pray,

You will never in your lifetime

face another hopeless day.

*Great* is the power of might and mind,

But only love can make us kind,

And all we are or hope to be

Is empty pride and vanity.

If love is not a part of all,

The greatest man is very small.

*The* house of prayer is no farther away

Than the quiet spot where you kneel and pray.

For the heart is a temple when God is there

As we place ourselves in His loving care.

*Though* I cannot find Your hand

To lead me on to the promised land,

I still believe with all my being

Your hand is still there beyond my seeing.

$\mathcal{H}e$ lived in a palace on a mountain of gold,

Surrounded by riches and wealth untold,

Priceless possessions and treasures of art,

But he died alone of a hungry heart

For man cannot live by bread alone

No matter what he may have or own,

For though he reaches his earthly goal,

He'll waste away with a starving soul

But he who eats of the holy bread

Will always find his spirit fed,

And even the poorest of men can afford

To feast at the table prepared by the Lord.

*Help* us, dear God,

to choose between

The driving forces that rule our routine

So we may make our purpose and goal

Not power and wealth

but the growth of our souls. . .

And give us strength and drive and desire

To raise our standards and ethics higher,

So all of us and not just a few

May live on earth as You want us to.

*Across* the years, we've met in dreams

And shared each other's hopes and schemes.

We've known a friendship rich and rare

And beautiful beyond compare. . .

But you reached out your arms for more

To catch what you were yearning for,

But little did you think or guess

That one can't capture happiness

Because it's unrestrained and free,

Unfettered by reality.

*It's* been many years since you both said "I do,"

And surely lots has happened to both of you,

For you can't live together for all of those years

And never dampen your smiles

    with at least a few tears. . .

And only through years of patience and sharing

Do you earn the priceless and rich joy of caring.

And these happy years so devotedly spent

Now bring you a harvest of peace and content.

*Kindness* is a virtue given by the Lord—

It pays dividends in happiness and joy is its reward.

For if you practice kindness in all you say and do,

The Lord will wrap His kindness

around your heart and you.

*Faith* is a force that is greater

than knowledge or power or skill,

And the darkest defeat turns to triumph

if you  trust in God's wisdom and will,

For faith is a mover of mountains—

there's nothing man cannot achieve

If he has the courage to try it

and then has the faith to believe.

*Through* long hours of tribulation

God gives us time for meditation,

And no sickness can be counted loss

That teaches us to bear our cross.

*God* seems much closer and needed much more

When trouble and sorrow stand outside our door,

For then we seek shelter in His wondrous love,

And we ask Him to send us help from above.

So we may know God better

    and feel His quiet power,

Let us daily keep in silence a meditation hour. . .

For to understand God's greatness

    and to use His gifts each day,

The soul must learn to meet Him in a meditative way.

*All* who believe in the risen Lord

Have been assured of this reward,

And death for them is just graduation

To a higher realm of wide elevation.

He hears every prayer and answers each one
When we pray in His name, "Thy will be done."
And the burdens that seemed too heavy to bear
Are lifted away on the wings of prayer.

*It's* true we have never looked on His face,

But His likeness shines forth from every place,

For the hand of God is everywhere

Along life's busy thoroughfare,

And His presence can be felt and seen

Right in the midst of our daily routine.

Things we touch and see and feel

Are what make God so very real.

*There* is nothing we need know

If we have faith that wherever we go

God will be there to help us to bear

Our disappointments, pain, and care,

For He is our Shepherd,

    our Father, our Guide,

And you're never alone

    with the Lord at your side.

*He* lives in the beauty that comes with spring—

The Easter lilies, the birds that sing—

And He lives in people as nice as you,

And He lives in all the nice things you do.

*In* the beauty of a snowflake

falling softly on the land

Is the mystery and the miracle

of God's great, creative hand.

What better answers are there

to prove His holy being

Than the wonders all around us

that are ours just for the seeing?

*We* know life's never measured

by how many years we live

But by the kindly things we do

and the happiness we give.

*Like* ships upon the sea of life

We meet with friends so dear,

Then sail on swiftly from the ones

We'd like to linger near;

Sometimes I wish

The winds would cease,

The waves be quiet, too,

And let me sort of drift along

Beside a friend like you.

God's love is like an island
in life's ocean vast and wide—
A peaceful, quiet shelter
from the restless, rising tide.
God's love is like an anchor
when the angry billows roll—
A mooring in the storms of life,
a stronghold for the soul.
God's love is like a fortress,
and we seek protection there

When the waves of tribulation

    seem to drown us in despair.

God's love is like a harbor

    where our souls can find sweet rest

From the struggle and the tension

    of life's fast and futile quest.

God's love is like a beacon

    burning bright with faith and prayer,

And through the changing scenes of life,

    we can find a haven there.

*Most* of the battles of life are won

By looking beyond the clouds to the sun

And having the patience to wait for the day

When the sun comes out and the clouds float away.

*Thank* God for the good things

He has already done,

And be grateful to Him for

the battles you've won—

And know that the same God

who helped you before

Is ready and willing

to help you once more.

*He's* ever-present and always there

To take you in His tender care

And bind the wounds and mend the breaks

When all the world around forsakes.

Somebody cares and loves you still,

And God is the someone who always will.

*Death* is not sad—it's time for elation,

A joyous transition, the soul's emigration

Into a place where the soul's safe and free

To live with God through eternity.

God's love is like a sanctuary

    where our souls can find sweet rest

From the struggle and the tension

    of life's fast and futile quest.

God's love is like a tower rising

    far above the crowd,

And God's smile is like the sunshine

    breaking through the threatening cloud.

*Life* is a mixture of sunshine and rain,

Good things and bad things, pleasure and pain.

We can't have all sunshine, but it's certainly true

That there's never a cloud

    the sun doesn't shine through. . .

So always remember, whatever betide you,

The power of God is always beside you.

*The* waking earth in springtime

Reminds us it is true

That nothing ever really dies

That is not born anew.

*If* people like me didn't know people like you,

Life would lose its meaning and its richness, too. . .

For the friends that we make are life's gift of love,

And I think friends are sent right from heaven above. . .

And thinking of you somehow makes me feel

That God is love and He's very real.

*Nothing* is ever too hard to do

If your faith is strong and your purpose is true. . .

So never give up, and never stop—

Just journey on to the mountaintop!

*Father*, make us kind and wise

So we may always recognize

The blessings that are ours to take,

The friendships that are ours to make.

*Death* is only a stepping stone

To a beautiful life we have never known—

A place where God promised man he would be

Eternally happy and safe and free.

*It's* never enough to seek God in prayer

With no thought of others who are lost in despair.

So teach us, dear God, that the power of prayer

Is made stronger by placing the world in Your care.

*We* cannot see the future,

    what's beyond is still unknown,

For the secret of God's kingdom

    still belongs to Him alone.

But He granted us salvation

    when His Son was crucified,

For life became immortal

    because our Savior died.

If you are searching to find the way
To life everlasting and eternal day,
With faith in your heart take the path that He trod,
For the way of the cross is the way to God.

*I am* the Way,

   so just follow Me

Though the way be rough

   and you cannot see. . .

I am the Truth

   which all men seek,

So heed not false prophets

   nor the words that they speak. . .

I am the Life,

    and I hold the key

That opens the door

    to eternity. . .

And in this dark world,

    I am the Light

To the promised land

    where there is no night.

He will not let me go alone
Into the valley that's unknown. . .
So I reach out and take Death's hand
And journey to the promised land.

*Memories* are treasures

that time cannot destroy,

They are the happy pathway

to yesterday's bright joy.

*Don't* start your day by supposin'

that trouble is just ahead—

It's better to stop supposin'

and start with a prayer instead.

*Oh* teach me, dear God, to not rush ahead,

But to pray for Your guidance and to trust You instead. . .

For You know what I need and that I'm only a slave

To the things that I want and desire and crave.

*A baby* is a gift of life

born of the wonder of love—

A little bit of eternity sent from

the Father above,

Giving a new dimension to the love

between husband and wife

And putting an added new meaning

to the wonder and mystery of life.

*Show* me the way to joy without end

With You as my Father, Redeemer, and Friend,

And send me the things that are hardest to bear,

And keep me forever safe in Thy care.

*No* life is worth living

unless it's built on truth,

And we lay our life's foundation

in the golden years of youth. . .

So allow no one to stop you

or hinder you from laying

A firm and strong foundation

made of faith and love and praying.

*I have* prayed in a velvet, hushed forest

where the quietness calmed my fears—

I have prayed through suffering and heartache

when my eyes were blinded with tears.

*Happiness* is something

    we create in our minds—

It's not something you search for and so seldom find.

It's just waking up and beginning the day

By counting our blessings and kneeling to pray.

*Show* me the way not to fortune and fame

Not how to win laurels or praise for my name,

But show me the way to spread the great story

That Thine is the kingdom

and power and glory.

*May* God bless your wedding day

and every day thereafter

And fill your home with happiness

and your hearts with love and laughter. . .

And may each year together

find you more and more in love

And bring you all the happiness

    you're so deserving of.

May the joy of true companionship

    be yours to share through life,

And may you always bless the day

    that made you husband and wife.

*The* years have never lessened

the longing in my heart

That came the day I realized

that we must dwell apart,

And just as long as memory lives,

my mother cannot die,

For in my heart she's living still

as passing years go by.

*If* you carve your name right in a man's heart

With a kindly word and a laugh

You can be mighty sure that your tombstone

Will be carved with the right epitaph.

*We* all need short vacations

   in life's fast and maddening race—

An interlude of quietness

   from the constant, jet-age pace,

So when your day is pressure-packed

   and your hours are all too few

Just close your eyes and meditate

   and let God talk to you.

*Love* is enduring and patient and kind—

It judges all with the heart, not with the mind. . .

And love can transform the most commonplace

Into beauty and splendor

and sweetness and grace.

To be in God's keeping is surely a blessing,

For though life is often dark and distressing,

No day is too dark and no burden too great

That God in His love cannot penetrate.

*My* garden beautifies my yard

    and adds fragrance to the air,

But it is also my cathedral

    and my quiet place of prayer.

So little do we realize that the glory

    and the power

Of Him who made the universe

    lies hidden in a flower!

*When* everything is quiet
and we're lost in meditation,
Our souls are then preparing
for a deeper dedication
That will make it wholly possible
to quietly endure
The violent world around us,
for in God we are secure.

*Silently* the green leaves grow,

In silence falls the soft, white snow,

Silently the flowers bloom,

In silence sunshine fills a room—

Silently bright stars appear,

In silence velvet night draws near,

And silently God enters in

To free a troubled heart from sin. . .

For God works silently in lives.

*God,* teach me to be patient,

teach me to go slow—

Teach me how to wait on You

when my way I do not know.

Teach me to let go, dear God,

and pray undisturbed until

My heart is filled with inner peace

and I learn to know Your will.

*Although* it sometimes seems to us

our prayers have not been heard,

God always knows our every need

without a single word,

And He will not forsake us even though

the way is steep,

For always He is near to us,

a tender watch to keep.

*Remember* me, God?

 I come every day

Just to talk with You, Lord,

 and to learn how to pray.

You make me feel welcome,

 You reach out Your hand.

I need never explain,

 for You understand.

*Suddenly,* Lord, I'm no longer afraid—

My burden is lighter and the dark shadows fade.

Oh God, what a comfort to know that You care

And to know when I seek You,

    You will always be there.

*Take* me and break me and make me,

    dear God, just what You want me to be.

Give me the strength to accept what You send

    and eyes with the vision to see

All the small, arrogant ways that I have

    and the vain little things that I do.

Make me aware that I'm often concerned

    more with myself than with You.

*Though* we are incapable,

    God's powerful and great,

And there's no darkness of the mind

    God cannot penetrate. . .

And all that is required of us

    whenever things go wrong

Is to trust in God implicitly

    with a faith that's deep and strong.

If you'll only try it, you will find,
 without a doubt,
A cheerful attitude's something
 no one should be without,
For when the heart is cheerful,
 it cannot be filled with fear,
And without fear, the way ahead
 seems more distinct and clear,
And we realize there's nothing
 that we must face alone,
For our heavenly Father loves us,
 and our problems are His own.

*I come* not to ask, to plead, or implore You—

I just come to tell You how much I adore You.

For to kneel in Your presence makes me feel blessed,

For I know that You know all my needs best,

And it fills me with joy just to linger with You,

As my soul You replenish and my heart You renew.

*God,* help me in my feeble way
To somehow do something each day
To show You that I love You best
And that my faith will stand each test,
And let me serve You every day
And feel You near me when I pray.
Oh, hear my prayer, dear God above,
And make me worthy of Your love.

*God,* open my eyes so I may see

And feel Your presence close to me.

Give me strength for my stumbling feet

As I battle the crowd on life's busy street,

And widen the vision of my unseeing eyes

So in passing faces I'll recognize

Not just a stranger, unloved and unknown,

But a friend with a heart that is much like my own.

*It* takes a mother's kindness

  to forgive us when we err,

To sympathize in trouble

  and to bow her head in prayer.

It takes a mother's wisdom

  to recognize our needs

And to give us reassurance

  by her loving words and deeds.

*God,* be my resting place and my protection

In hours of trouble, defeat, and dejection—

May I never give way to self-pity and sorrow,

May I always be sure of a better tomorrow.

*May* I stand undaunted come what may,

Secure in the knowledge I have only to pray

And ask my Creator and Father above

To keep me serene in His grace and His love.

*Dear* God, You are a part of me—

You're all I do and all I see,

You're what I say and what I do,

For all my life belongs to You.

You walk with me and talk with me,

For I am Yours eternally.

*Good* health, good humor,

And good sense,

No one is poor

With this defense.

*I cannot* dwell apart from You—
You would not ask or want me to,
For You have room within Your heart
To make each child of Yours a part
Of You and all Your love and care
If we but come to You in prayer.

*Bless* me, heavenly Father,

forgive my erring ways.

Grant me strength to serve Thee;

put purpose in my days.

Help me when I falter

and hear me when I pray,

And receive me in Thy kingdom

to dwell with Thee someday.

*When* your heart is heavy

    and your day is dull with care,

Instead of trying to escape,

    why not withdraw in prayer?

For when we go to God in prayer,

    our thoughts are rearranged,

So even though our problems have not

    been solved or changed,

Somehow the good Lord gives us

    the power to understand

That He who holds tomorrow

    is the One who holds our hands.

*After* winter comes the spring

To breathe new life in everything,

And all the flowers that fell in death

Will be awakened by spring's breath. . .

For in God's plan both men and flowers

Can only reach bright, shining hours

By dying first to rise in glory

And prove again the Easter story.

*There* is only one place and only one friend

Who is never too busy, and you can always depend

On Him to be waiting, with arms open wide

To hear all the troubles you came to confide. . .

For the heavenly Father will always be there

When you seek Him and find Him

    at the altar of prayer.

The priceless gift of life is love,

For with the help of God above

Love can change the human race

And make this world a better place...

For love dissolves all hate and fear

And makes our vision bright and clear

So we can see and rise above

Our pettiness on wings of love.

*Only* through prayer that's unhurried

    can the needs of the day be met

And only through prayers said at evening

    can we sleep without fears or regret.

So seek the Lord in the morning

    and never forget Him at night,

For prayer is an unfailing blessing

    that makes every burden seem light.

*Whenever* I am troubled and lost in deep despair,

I bundle all my troubles up and go to God in prayer. . .

I know He stilled the tempest and calmed the angry sea,

And I humbly ask if, in His love,

   He'll do the same for me. . .

And then I just keep quiet

   and think only thoughts of peace,

And if I abide in stillness my restless murmurings cease.

*In* Thy goodness and mercy,

    look down on this weak, erring one

And tell me that I am forgiven

    for all I've so willfully done,

And teach me to humbly start following

    the path  that the dear Savior trod

So I'll find at the end of life's journey

    a home in the city of God.

*Start* every day with a "good morning" prayer

And God will bless each thing you do

and keep you in His care. . .

And never, never sever the spirit's silken strand

That our Father up in heaven

holds in His mighty hand.

*We* are weak and wavering,

uncertain and unsure,

And only meeting You in prayer

can help us to endure

All life's trials and troubles,

its sickness, pain, and sorrow

And give us strength and courage

to face and meet tomorrow.

*The* love of God surrounds us

Like the air we breathe around us—

As near as a heartbeat, as close as a prayer,

And whenever we need Him,

   He'll always be there!

*There's* no problem too big

    and no question too small—

Just ask God in faith and He'll answer them all—

Not always at once, so be patient and wait,

For God never comes too soon or too late. . .

So trust in His wisdom

    and believe in His word,

For no prayer's unanswered

    and no prayer's unheard.

*Prayers* are the stairs that lead to God,

and there's joy every step of the way

When we make our pilgrimage to Him

with love in our hearts each day.

*On* the wings of prayer our burdens take flight

And our load of care becomes bearably light

And our heavy hearts are lifted above

To be healed by the balm

    of God's wonderful love.

*God's* presence is ever beside you,

as near as the reach of your hand.

You have but to tell Him your troubles—

there is nothing He won't understand. . .

And knowing God's love is unfailing,

and His mercy unending and great,

You have but to trust in His promise—

"God comes not too soon or too late."

*Often* we pause and wonder
   when we kneel down and pray
Can God really hear the prayers that we say?
But if we keep praying and talking to Him,
He'll brighten the soul that was clouded and dim
And as we continue, our burden seems lighter,
Our sorrow is softened and our outlook is brighter.

*Whenever* we're troubled and lost in despair,

We have but to seek Him and ask Him in prayer

To guide and direct us and help us to bear

Our sickness and sorrow, our worry and care.

*Just* close your eyes and open your heart

And feel your cares and worries depart.

Just yield yourself to the Father above

And let Him hold you secure in His love.

*They* tell me that prayer

helps to quiet the mind

And to unburden the heart,

for in stillness we find

A newborn assurance that

someone does care

And someone does answer

each small, sincere prayer.

*The* house of prayer is no farther away

Than the quiet spot where you kneel and pray.

For the heart is a temple when God is there

As we place ourselves

in His loving care.

*God* is already deeply aware

Of the burdens we find too heavy to bear. . .

And all we need do is seek Him in prayer

And without a word He will help us to bear

Our trials and troubles, our sickness and sorrow

And show us the way to a brighter tomorrow.

*The* more you give, the more you get—

The more you laugh, the less you fret.

The more you do unselfishly,

The more you live abundantly—

The more of everything you share,

The more you'll always have to spare.

The more you love, the more you'll find

That life is good and friends are kind,

For only what we give away

Enriches us from day to day.

*God* of love, forgive—forgive.

Teach me how to truly live.

Ask me not my race or creed,

Just take me in my hour of need

And let me know You love me, too,

And that I am a part of You.

*Someday* may man realize

That all the earth, the seas, and skies

Belong to God, who made us all—

The rich, the poor, the great, the small—

And in the Father's holy sight

No man is yellow, black, or white. . .

And peace on earth cannot be found

Until we meet on common ground

And every man becomes a brother

Who worships God and loves each other.

*Kneel* in prayer in His presence

and you'll find no need to speak,

For softly in quiet communion,

God grants you the peace that you seek.

*My* cross is not too heavy,

my road is not too rough

Because God walks beside me,

and to know this is enough. . .

And though I get so lonely,

I know I'm not alone,

For the Lord God is my Father

and He loves me as His own.

*Brighten* your day

And lighten your way

And lessen your cares

With daily prayers.

Quiet your mind

And leave tension behind

And find inspiration

In hushed meditation.

*No* one ever sought the Father

and found He was not there,

And no burden is too heavy

to be lightened by a prayer.

No problem is too intricate,

and no sorrow that we face

Is too deep and devastating

to be softened by His grace.

*His* love knows no exceptions,

    so never feel excluded—

No matter who or what you are,

    your name has been included. . .

And no matter what your past has been,

    trust God to understand,

And no matter what your problem is,

    just place it in His hand. . .

For in all our unloveliness this great

    God loves us still—

He loved us since the world began,

    and what's more, He always will!

*No* trials and tribulations are beyond

   what we can bear

If we share them with our Father

   as we talk to Him in prayer. . .

And men of every color, every race,

   and every creed

Have but to seek the Father

   in their deepest hour of need.

*There* are many things in life

we cannot understand,

But we must trust God's judgment

and be guided by His hand. . .

And all who have God's blessing

can rest safely in His care,

For He promises safe passage

on the wings of faith and prayer.

*Prayer* is much more than just asking for things—

It's the peace and contentment that quietness brings.

So thank You again for Your mercy and love

And for making me heir to Your kingdom above.

It's amazing and incredible,

but it's as true as it can be—

God loves and understands us all,

and that means you and me.

His grace is all-sufficient for both

the young and old,

For the lonely and the timid,

for the brash and for the bold.

*Let* me stop complaining

    about my load of care,

For God will always lighten it

    when it gets too much to bear. . .

And if He does not ease my load,

    He'll give me strength to bear it,

For God, in love and mercy,

    is always near to share it.

*My* blessings are so many,

my troubles are so few—

How can I be discouraged

when I know that I have You?

And I have the sweet assurance

that there's nothing I need fear

If I but keep remembering

I am Yours and You are near.

*God's* love endures forever—

    what a wonderful thing to know

When the tides of life run against you

    and your spirit is downcast and low.

God's kindness is ever around you

    always ready to freely impart

Strength to your faltering spirit,

    cheer to your lonely heart.

*When* life seems empty and there's no place to go,

When you heart is troubled and your spirits are low,

When friends seem few and nobody cares—

There is always God to hear your prayers.

*The* burden that seems too heavy to bear

God lifts away on the wings of prayer. . .

And seen through God's eyes earthly troubles diminish

And we're given new strength to face and to finish

Life's daily tasks as they come along

If we pray for strength to keep us strong. . .

So go to our Father when troubles assail you,

For His grace is sufficient

and He'll never fail you.

*Tender* little memories of some word or deed

Give us strength and courage when we are in need.

Blessed little memories help us bear the cross

And soften all the bitterness of failure and loss.

Precious little memories of little things we've done

Make the very darkest day a bright and happy one.

*As* we pray for guidance, may a troubled world revive

Faith in God and confidence so our nation may survive,

And draw us ever closer to God and to each other

Until every stranger is a friend and every man a brother.

*Somebody* loves you more than you know,

Somebody goes with you wherever you go,

Somebody really and truly cares

And lovingly listens to all of your prayers.

*Trust* in His wisdom and follow His ways

And be not concerned with the world's empty praise,

But first seek His kingdom and you will possess

The world's greatest of riches, which is true happiness.

*When* you're troubled

　　and worried and sick at heart

And your plans are upset

　　and your world falls apart,

Remember God's ready

　　and waiting to share

The burden you find

　　too heavy to bear.

*I meet* God in the morning

and go with Him through the day,

Then in the stillness of the night

before sleep comes I pray

That God will just take over

all the problems I couldn't solve,

And in the peacefulness of sleep

my cares will all dissolve.

*I have* prayed on my knees in the morning,

I have prayed as I walked along,

I have prayed in the silence and darkness,

and I've prayed to the tune of a song.

*Never,* never discount what God
has promised man
If he will walk in meekness
and accept God's flawless plan,
For if we heed His teaching
as we journey through the years,
We'll find the richest jewels of all
are crystallized from tears.

*We* are all God's children and He loves us, every one.

He freely and completely forgives all that we have done,

Asking only if we're ready to follow where He leads,

Content that in His wisdom He will answer all our needs.

*This* brings you a million good wishes and more

For the things you cannot buy in a store—

Like faith to sustain you in times of trial,

A joy-filled heart and a happy smile,

Contentment, inner peace, and love—

All priceless gifts from God above!

*Everyone* needs someone to be thankful for,

And each day of life we are aware of this more,

For the joy of enjoying and the fullness of living

Are found only in hearts that are filled

with thanksgiving.

"*Love* one another, as I have loved you"

May seem impossible to do,

But if you will try to trust and believe,

Great are the joys that you will receive.

*As* soon as love entered the heart's open door,

The faults we once saw are not there anymore—

And the things that seem wrong begin to look right

When viewed in the softness of love's gentle light.

*Whatever* is wrong with your life today,

You'll find a solution if you kneel down and pray

Not just for pleasure, enjoyment, and health,

Not just for honors, prestige, and wealth,

But pray for a purpose to make life worth living,

And pray for the joy of unselfish giving...

For great is your gladness

 and rich your reward

When you make your life's purpose

 the choice of the Lord.

*Love* works in ways that are wondrous and strange,

And there is nothing in life that love cannot change,

And all that God promised will someday come true

When you have loved one another the way He loved you.

*He's* the stars in the heavens, a smile on some face,

A leaf on a tree or a rose in a vase.

He's winter and autumn and summer and spring—

In short, God is every real, wonderful thing.

I wish I might meet Him much more than I do—

I would if there were more people like you.

*Some* folks call it fickle fate

and some folks call it chance

While others just accept it

as a pleasant happenstance,

But no matter what you call it,

it didn't come without design,

For all our lives are fashioned

by the hand that is divine

And every lucky happening

and every lucky break

Are little gifts from God above

that are ours to freely take.

In a myriad of miraculous ways

God shapes our lives and changes our days.

Beyond our will or even knowing

God keeps our spirits ever growing.

*On* the wings of loss and pain,

The peace we often sought in vain

Will come to us with sweet surprise,

For God is merciful and wise. . .

And through dark hours of tribulation

God gives us time for meditation,

And nothing can be counted loss

Which teaches us to bear our cross.

*God* is no stranger in a faraway place—

He's as close as the wind that blows 'cross my face.

It's true I can't see the wind as it blows,

But I feel it around me and my heart surely knows

That God's mighty hand can be felt everywhere,

For there's nothing on earth that is not in God's care.

*The* sky and the stars,

    the waves and the sea,

The dew on the grass,

    the leaves on a tree

Are constant reminders of God

    and His nearness

Proclaiming His presence

    with crystal-like clearness.

*How* could I think God

was far, far away

When I feel Him beside me

every hour of the day?

And I've plenty of reasons

to know God's my friend,

And this is one friendship

that time cannot end.

*Each* day there are showers of blessings
sent from the Father above,
For God is a great, lavish giver,
and there is no end to His love. . .
And His grace is more than sufficient,
His mercy is boundless and deep,
And His infinite blessings are countless—
and all this we're given to keep.

*No* matter how big man's dreams are,

God's blessings are infinitely more,

For always God's giving is greater

than what man is asking for.

*When* you're overwhelmed with fears

And all your hopes are drenched in tears,

Think not that life has been unfair

And given you too much to bear,

For God has chosen you because,

With all your weaknesses and flaws,

He feels that you are worthy of

The greatness of His wondrous love.

If everybody brightened up
the spot on which they're standing
By being more considerate
and a little less demanding,
This dark old world would very soon
eclipse the evening star
If everybody brightened up
the corner where they are.

*In* this troubled world it's refreshing to find

Someone who still has the time to be kind,

Someone who still has the faith to believe

That the more that you give, the more you receive,

Someone who's ready by thought, word, or deed

To reach out a hand in the hour of need.

*If* we would but forget our care

And stop in sympathy to share

The burden that our brother carried,

Our minds and hearts would be less harried

And we would feel our load was small—

In fact, we carried no load at all.

$It's$ a wonderful world,

   and it's people like you

Who make it that way

   by the things that they do.

For a warm, ready smile or a kind,

   thoughtful deed

Or a hand outstretched

   in an hour of need

Can change our whole outlook

   and make the world bright

Where a minute before just nothing seemed right.

It's a wonderful world and it always will be

If we keep our eyes open and focused to see

The wonderful things we are capable of

When we open our hearts

  to God and His love.

*Somebody* cares and always will—

The world forgets, but God loves you still

You cannot go beyond His love

No matter what you're guilty of,

For God forgives until the end—

He is your faithful, loyal friend.

*Time* is not measured by the years that you live

But by the deeds that you do and the joy that you give.

And each day as it comes brings a chance to each one

To live to the fullest, leaving nothing undone

So what does it matter how long we may live

If as long as we live we unselfishly give.

*You* can't do a kindness without a reward—

Not in silver or gold but in joy from the Lord.

You can't light a candle to show others the way

Without feeling the warmth of that bright little ray,

And you can't pluck a rose all fragrant with dew

Without part of its fragrance remaining with you.

*Life* is a highway on which the years go by,

Sometimes the road is level,

   sometimes the hills are high. . .

But as we travel onward to a future that's unknown,

We can make each mile we travel

   a heavenly stepping stone!

*Teach* me to give of myself in whatever way I can,

of whatever I have to give.

Teach me to value myself—my time, my talents,

my purpose, my life, my meaning in Your world.

*Only* what we give away
Enriches us from day to day,
For not in getting but in giving
Is found the lasting joy of living,
For no one ever had a part
In sharing treasures of the heart
Who did not feel the impact of
The magic mystery of God's love.

*Make* me a channel of blessing today—

I ask again and again when I pray.

Do I turn a deaf ear to the Master's voice

Or refuse to hear His direction and choice?

I only know at the end of the day

That I did so little to pay my way.

It's not fortune or fame or worldwide acclaim

That makes for true greatness, you'll find

It's the wonderful art of teaching the heart

To always be thoughtful and kind!

*A kind* and thoughtful deed

Or a hand outstretched in a time of need

Is the rarest of gifts, for it is a part

Not of the purse but of a loving heart. . .

And he who gives of himself will find

True joy of heart and peace of mind.

*It's* not the things that can be bought

That are life's richest treasures,

It's just the little "heart gifts"

That money cannot measure—

A cheerful smile, a friendly word,

A sympathetic nod,

All priceless little treasures

From the storehouse

   of our God.

*There's* truly nothing we need know

If we have faith wherever we go,

God will be there to help us bear

Our disappointments, pain, and care,

For He is our shepherd, our Father, our guide—

You're never alone with the Lord at your side.

*When* we bring some pleasure

to another human heart,

We have followed in His footsteps

and we've had a little part

In serving God who loves us—

for I'm very sure it's true

That in serving those around us,

we serve and please God, too.

*At* times like these

man is helpless. . .

it is only God

who can speak the words

that calm the sea,

still the wind,

and ease the pain. . .

so lean on Him

and you will never walk alone.

*Spare* me no heartache or sorrow, dear Lord,

For the heart that hurts reaps the richest reward,

And God blesses the heart that is broken with sorrow

As He opens the door to a brighter tomorrow. . .

For only through tears can we recognize

The suffering that lies in another's eyes.

*Things* achieved too easily
    lose their charm and meaning, too,
For it is life's difficulties
    and the trial times we go through
That make us strong in spirit
    and endow us with the will
To surmount the insurmountable
    and to climb the highest hill.

*Cheerful* thoughts like sunbeams

lighten up the darkest fears,

For when the heart is happy

there's just no time for tears,

And when the face is smiling

it's impossible to frown,

And when you are high-spirited

you cannot feel low-down.

*Cast* your burden on Him,

    seek His counsel when distressed,

And go to Him for comfort

    when you're lonely and oppressed. . .

For in God is our encouragement

    in trouble and in trials,

And in suffering and in sorrow

    He will turn our tears to smiles.

*Remember* when you're troubled

     with uncertainty and doubt,

It is best to tell our Father

     what our fear is all about,

For unless we seek His guidance

     when troubled times arise,

We are bound to make decisions

     that are twisted and unwise,

But when we view our problems

     through the eyes of God above,

Misfortunes turn to blessings

     and hatred turns to love.

*Sometimes* the road of life seems long

   as we travel through the years

And with a heart that's broken and eyes brimful of tears,

We falter in our weariness and sink beside the way,

But God leans down and whispers,

   "Child, there'll be another day,"

And the road will grow much smoother

   and much easier to face,

So do not be disheartened—this is just a resting place.

*In* sickness or health,

In suffering and pain,

In storm-laden skies,

In sunshine and rain,

God always is there

To lighten your way

And lead you through darkness

To a much brighter day.

*Sometimes* we come to life's crossroads

and view what we think is the end,

But God has a much wider vision,

and He knows it's only a bend—

The road will go on and get smoother,

and after we've stopped for a rest,

The path that lies hidden beyond us

    is often the part that is best. . .

So rest and relax and grow stronger—

    let go and let God share your load,

And have faith in a brighter tomorrow—

    you've just come to a bend in the road.

*The* more we endure with patience and grace,

The stronger we grow and the more we can face—

And the more we can face, the greater our love,

And with love in our hearts we are more conscious of

The pain and the sorrow in lives everywhere—

So it is through trouble that we learn to share.

*A wish* that's sent with lots of love

Just seems to have a feeling—

A special word of sentiment

That makes it more appealing.

And that's the kind of loving wish

That's being sent your way

To hope that every day will be

Your happy kind of day.

*Oh* God, look down on our cold hearts

and warm them with Your love,

And grant us Your forgiveness

which we're so unworthy of.

*Waste* no time in crying

    on the shoulder of a friend,

But go directly to the Lord,

    for on Him you can depend. . .

For there's absolutely nothing

    that His mighty hand can't do,

And He never is too busy

    to help and comfort you.

On the wings of death and sorrow

God sends us new hope for tomorrow,

And in His mercy and His grace

He gives us strength to bravely face

The lonely days that stretch ahead

And to know our loved one is not dead

But only sleeping out of our sight,

And we'll meet in that land where there is no night.

Let me say no to the flattery and praise

And quietly spend the rest of my days

Far from the greed and the speed of man,

Who has so distorted God's simple life plan,

And let me be great in the eyes of You, Lord,

For that is the richest, most priceless reward.

If I can but keep on believing what I know
in my heart to be true,
That darkness will fade with the morning
and that this will pass away, too—
Then nothing in life can defeat me,
for as long as this knowledge remains,

I can suffer whatever is happening,

    for I know God will break all the chains

That are binding me tight in the darkness

    and trying to fill me with fear. . .

For there is no night without dawning,

    and I know that my morning is near.

$It$ doesn't take a new year

   to begin our lives anew—

God grants us new beginnings each day

   the whole year through.

So never be discouraged,

   for there comes daily to all men

The chance to make another start

   and begin all over again.

*While* life's springtime is sweet to recall,

The autumn of life is the best time of all,

For our wild youthful yearnings all gradually cease

And God fills our days

   with beauty and peace!

God never plows in the soul of man

Without intention and purpose and plan. . .

So whenever you feel the plow's sharp blade

Let not your heart be sorely afraid,

For like the farmer, God chooses a field

From which He expects an excellent yield. . .

So rejoice though your heart be broken in two—

God seeks to bring forth a rich harvest in you.

*Blessings* come in many guises
That God alone in love devises,
And sickness, which we dread so much,
Can bring a very healing touch,
For often on the wings of pain
The peace we sought before in vain
Will come to us with sweet surprise,
For God is merciful and wise.

*After* the clouds, the sunshine,

After the winter, the spring,

After the shower, the rainbow—

For life is a changeable thing.

After the night, the morning

Bidding all darkness cease,

After life's cares and sorrows,

The comfort and sweetness of peace.

*The* faith to endure whatever comes

is born of sorrow and trials

And strengthened only by discipline

and nurtured by self-denials. . .

So be not disheartened by troubles,

for trials are the building blocks

On which to erect a fortress of faith,

secure on God's ageless rocks.

*While* it's very difficult

for mankind to understand

God's intentions and His purpose

and the workings of His hand,

God makes what seemed unbearable

and painful and distressing

Easily acceptable when we

view it as a blessing.

If we open the door to let joy walk through

When we learn to expect the best and the most, too,

And believing we'll find a happy surprise

Makes reality out of a fancied surmise.

*God* gives us a power

    we so seldom employ

For we're so unaware

    it is filled with such joy.

The gift that God gives us

    is anticipation,

Which we can fulfill

    with sincere expectation,

For there's power in belief

    when we think we will find

Joy for the heart

    and peace for the mind.

*Our* Father knows what's best for us,

    so why should we complain—

We always want the sunshine,

    but He knows there must be rain—

We love the sound of laughter

    and the merriment of cheer,

But our hearts would lose their tenderness

    if we never shed a tear. . .

So whenever we are troubled

    and life has lost its song

It's God testing us with burdens

    just to make our spirit strong.

*Whether* God answers promptly

   or delays in answering your prayer,

You must have faith to believe Him

   and to know in your heart He'll be there.

So be not impatient or hasty,

   just trust in the Lord and believe,

For whatever you ask in faith and love,

   in abundance you are sure to receive.

*Take* heart and meet each minute

with faith in God's great love,

Aware that every day of life

is controlled by God above. . .

And never dread tomorrow

or what the future brings—

Just pray for strength and courage

and trust God in all things.

*All* we really ever need

Is faith as a grain of mustard seed,

For all God asks is, "Do you believe?"

For if you do ye shall receive.

"*Do* justice"—"Love kindness"—

"Walk humbly with God"—

For with these three things as your rule and your rod,

All things worth having are yours to achieve,

If you follow God's words and have faith to believe.

*Tiny* hands and tousled heads

That kneel in prayer by little beds

Are closer to the dear Lord's heart

And of His kingdom more a part

Than we who search and never find

The answers to our questioning minds—

For faith in things we cannot see

Requires a child's simplicity.

*The* wise man accepts whatever God sends,

Willing to yield like a storm-tossed tree bends,

Knowing that God never made a mistake,

So whatever He sends they are willing to take...

For trouble is part and parcel of life,

And no man can grow without struggle or strife.

*There* is really nothing we need know

    or even try to understand

If we refuse to be discouraged

    and trust God's guiding hand,

So take heart and meet each minute

    with faith in God's great love,

Aware that every day of life

    is controlled by God above.

*Never* dread tomorrow or what the future brings

Just pray for strength and courage

and trust God in all things,

And never grow discouraged—

be patient and just wait,

For God never comes too early,

and He never comes too late.

*Love* is the language that every heart speaks,

For love is the one thing that every heart seeks. . .

And where there is love God, too, will abide

And bless the family residing inside.

"*Do* not be anxious," said our Lord,

"Have peace from day to day—

The lilies neither toil nor spin,

Yet none are clothed as they."

The meadowlark with sweetest song

Fears not for bread or nest

Because he trusts our Father's love

And God knows what is best.

*If* we place our lives in God's hands

And surrender completely to His will and demands,

The darkness lifts and the sun shines through,

And by His touch we are born anew.

*Always* remember, the hills ahead
are never as steep as they seem,
And with faith in your heart, start upward
and climb till you reach your dream.
For nothing in life that is worthy
is ever too hard to achieve
If you have the courage to try it
and you have the faith to believe.

*Dawn* cannot follow a night of despair

Unless faith lights a candle in all hearts everywhere. . .

And warmed by the glow, our hate melts away

And love lights the path to a peaceful new day.

*Faith* is a force that is greater

than knowledge or power or skill,

And many defeats turn to triumphs

if you trust in God's wisdom and will.

For faith is a mover of mountains—

there's nothing that God cannot do—

So start out today with faith in your heart

and climb till your dream comes true.

*It's* easy to grow downhearted
   when nothing goes your way,
It's easy to be discouraged
   when you have a troublesome day,
But trouble is only a challenge
   to spur you on to achieve
The best that God has to offer,
   if you have the faith to believe!

*Men* may misjudge you, but God's verdict is fair,

For He looks deep inside and is deeply aware

Of every small detail in your pattern of living,

And always He's fair and lenient

and forgiving.

*Be* glad that your life has been full and complete,

Be glad that you've tasted the bitter and sweet.

Be glad that you've walked in sunshine and rain,

Be glad that you've felt both pleasure and pain.

Be glad that you've had such a full, happy life,

Be glad for your joy as well as your strife.

Be glad that you've walked with courage each day,

Be glad you've had strength for each step of the way.

Be glad for the comfort

    that you've found in prayer.

Be glad for God's blessings,

    His love, and His care.

*Deal* only with the present—

never step into tomorrow,

For God asks us just to trust Him

and to never borrow sorrow,

For to meet tomorrow's troubles before

they are even ours

Is to anticipate the Savior

and to doubt His all-wise powers,

So let us be content to solve

our problems one by one,

Asking nothing of tomorrow except

"Thy will be done."

*What* a wonderful time is life's autumn,

    when the leaves of the trees are all gold,

When God fills each day as He sends it

    with memories, priceless and old.

What a treasure-house filled with rare jewels

    are the blessings of year upon year,

When life has been lived as you've lived it

    in a home where God's presence is near.

*At* this time we offer up a prayer

To thank You, God, for giving us

a lot more than our share.

First, thank You for the little things

that often come our way—

The things we take for granted

and don't mention when we pray—

The unexpected courtesy,

the thoughtful, kindly deed,

A hand reached out to help us

in the time of sudden need.

*Make* us more aware, dear God,

    of little daily graces

That come to us with sweet surprise

    from never-dreamed-of places.

Then thank You for the miracles

    we are much too blind to see,

And give us new awareness of our many gifts from Thee.

And help us to remember that the key to life and living

Is to make each prayer a prayer of thanks

    and each day a day of thanksgiving.

*Thank* You, God, for everything—

the big things and the small—

For every good gift comes from God,

the giver of them all.

*Memory* builds a little pathway

  that goes winding through my heart.

It's a lovely, quiet, gentle trail from other things apart.

I only meet when traveling there the folks I like the best,

For this road I call remembrance is hidden from the rest,

But I hope I'll always find you

  in my memory rendezvous,

For I keep this little secret place

  to meet with folks like you.

*The* good, green earth beneath our feet,

The air we breathe, the food we eat,

Some work to do, a goal to win,

A hidden longing deep within

That spurs us on to bigger things

And helps us meet what each day brings—

All these things and many more

Are things we should be thankful for. . .

And most of all, our thankful prayers

Should rise to God because He cares.

*Give* thanks for the blessings that daily are ours—
The warmth of the sun, the fragrance of flowers.
With thanks for all the thoughtful,
  caring things you always do
And a loving wish for happiness
  today and all year through!

*They* asked me how I know it's true

    that the Savior lived and died

And if I believe the story

    that the Lord was crucified. . .

And I have so many answers

    to prove His holy being—

Answers that are everywhere

    within the realm of seeing—

The leaves that fall in autumn

    and were buried in the sod

Now budding on the tree boughs

    to lift their arms to God,

The flowers that were covered

    and entombed beneath the snow

Pushing through the darkness

    to bid the spring hello.

On every side, great nature sings

    the Easter story,

So who am I to question

    the Resurrection glory?

*Let* us all remember

    when our faith is running low,

Christ is more than just a figure

    wrapped in an ethereal glow.

For He came and dwelled among us

    and He knows our every need,

And He loves and understands us

    and forgives each sinful deed.

*Our* Savior's resurrection

    was God's way of telling men

That in Christ we are eternal

    and in Him we live again. . .

And to know life is unending

    and God's love is endless, too,

Makes our daily tasks

    and burdens so much easier to do.

*No* matter how downhearted

and discouraged we may be,

New hope is born when we behold

leaves budding on a tree,

And troubles seem to vanish

when robins start to sing,

For God never sends the winter

without the joy of spring.

*There* can be no crown of stars

Without a cross to bear,

And there is no salvation

Without faith and love and prayer,

And when we take our needs to God

Let us pray as did His Son

That dark night in Gethsamane—

"Thy will, not mine, be done."

*Only* a child can completely accept

What probing adults research and reject.

O Father, grant once more to men

A simple, childlike faith again,

For only by faith and faith alone

Can we approach our Father's throne.

*When* I write your name I think of you

And pause and reflect and always renew

The bond that exists since we first met

And I found you somebody too nice to forget.

*Our* Father up in heaven,

long, long years ago,

Looked down in His great mercy

upon the earth below

And saw that folks were lonely

and lost in deep despair,

And so He said, "I'll send My Son

to walk among them there

So they can hear Him speaking and

feel His nearness, too,

And see the many miracles

that faith alone can do."

*Help* us when we falter and renew our faith each day

And forgive our human errors and hear us when we pray,

And keep us gently humble in the greatness of Thy love

So someday we are fit to dwell with Thee in peace above.

*May* you find rich satisfaction

In your daily work and prayer,

And in knowing as you serve Him

He will keep you in His care.

*Hope* to light our pathway

    when the way ahead is dark,

Hope to sing through stormy days

    with the sweetness of a lark,

Faith to trust in things unseen

    and know beyond all seeing

That it is in our Father's love we live

    and have our being,

And love to break down barriers

    of color, race, and creed,

Love to see and understand

    and help all those in need.

*Man,* with all his knowledge,

his wisdom, and his skill,

Is powerless to go beyond

the holy Father's will. . .

And when we fully recognize

the helplessness of man

and seek our Father's guidance

in our every thought and plan,

Then only can we build a world

of faith and hope and love,

And only then can man achieve

the life he's dreaming of.

*Only* because Christ was born and died

And hung on a cross to be crucified

Can worldly sinners like you and me

Be fit to live in eternity.

*There's* one rare and priceless gift

that can't be sold or bought—

It's something poor or rich can give,

for it's a loving thought...

And loving thoughts are blessings

for which no one can pay,

And only loving hearts can give

this priceless gift away.

*What* is love? No words can define it—

It's something so great only God could design it.

Wonder of wonders, beyond man's conception—

And only in God can love find true perfection.

*It* takes a special day like this

To just look back and reminisce

And think of things you've shared together

Through sunny, fair, and stormy weather,

And how both smiles as well as tears

Endear true love across the years. . .

For there is no explaining of

The mystery of the bond of love,

Which just grows richer, deeper, stronger

Because you've shared it

one year longer.

*I said* a Father's Day prayer for you—

    I asked the Lord above

To keep you safely in His care

    and enfold you in His love. . .

I did not ask for fortune, for riches, or for fame,

I only asked for blessings in the holy Savior's name—

Blessings to surround you in times of trial and stress,

And inner joy to fill your heart

    with peace and happiness.

*God,* in His wisdom and mercy,

  looked down on His children below

And gave them the privilege of choosing

  the right or the wrong way to go. . .

So trust in His almighty wisdom

  and enjoy the fruit of His love,

And life on earth will be happy

  as you walk with the Father above.

*We* all make mistakes—it's human to err—

But no one need ever give up in despair,

For God gives us all a brand-new beginning,

A chance to start over and repent of our sinning. . .

And when God forgives us, we, too, must forgive

And resolve to do better each day that we live.

*God's* love is like an island

in life's ocean vast and wide—

A peaceful, quiet shelter from

the restless, rising tide.

God's love is like a fortress,

and we seek protection there

When the waves of tribulation

seem to drown us in despair.

*Love* is like magic and it always will be,

For love still remains life's sweet mystery.

Love works in ways that are wondrous and strange,

And there's nothing in life

   that love cannot change.

*Where* there is love there is a smile

To make all things seem more worthwhile.

Where there is love there's a quiet peace—

A tranquil place where turmoils cease.

*Wish* not for the easy way

    to win your heart's desire,

For the joy's in overcoming

    and withstanding flood and fire,

For to triumph over trouble

    and grow stronger with defeat

Is to win the kind of victory

    that will make your life complete.

*Love* changes darkness into light
And makes the heart take wingless flight.
Oh, blessed are those who walk in love—
They also walk with God above.

*When* you walk with God each day

And kneel together when you pray,

Your marriage will be truly blessed

And God will be your daily guest,

And love that once seemed yours alone

God gently blends into His own.

*You're* lovable, you're wonderful,

You're as sweet as you can be,

There's nobody in all the world

Could mean so much to me;

I love you more than life itself,

You make my dreams come true,

Forever is not long enough

For me to be near to you.

*God* in His goodness has promised

   that the cross that He gives us to wear

Will never exceed our endurance

   or be more than our strength can bear. . .

And secure in that blessed assurance,

   we can smile as we face tomorrow,

For God holds the key to the future,

   and no sorrow or care we need borrow.

*Nothing* on earth or in heaven can part

A love that has grown to be part of the heart

And just like the sun and the stars and the sea,

This love will go on through eternity,

For true love lives on when earthly things die,

For it's part of the spirit that soars to the sky.

*You* cannot go beyond my thoughts

or leave my love behind

Because I keep you in my heart

and forever on my mind. . .

And though I may not tell you,

I think you know it's true

That I find daily happiness

in the very thought of you.

*Love* is unselfish, giving more than it takes—

And no matter what happens love never forsakes.

It's faithful and trusting and always believing,

Guileless and honest and never deceiving.

Yes, love is beyond what man can define,

For love is immortal and God's gift is divine!

*Life* is a garden, good friends are the flowers,

And times spent together life's happiest hours. . .

And friendship, like flowers, blooms ever more fair

When carefully tended by dear friends who care. . .

And life's lovely garden would be sweeter by far

If all who passed through it

were as nice as you are.

*Days* of wine and roses
      never make love's dreams come true—
It takes sacrifice and teardrops
      and problems shared by two
To give true love its beauty,
      its grandeur and its fineness,
And to mold an earthly ecstasy
      into heavenly divineness.

*When* we need some sympathy

    or a friendly hand to touch

Or one who listens and speaks words

    that mean so much,

We seek a true and trusted friend

    in the knowledge that we'll find

A heart that's sympathetic

    and an understanding mind. . .

And often just without a word

    there seems to be a union

Of thoughts and kindred feelings,

    for God gives true friends communion.

*God* knows no strangers, He loves us all,

The poor, the rich, the great, the small.

He is a friend who is always there

To share our troubles and lessen our care.

*Open* up your hardened hearts and let God enter in,

He only wants to help you a new life to begin,

And every day's a good day to lose yourself in others,

And any time's a good time to see mankind as brothers,

And this can only happen when you realize it's true

That everyone needs someone and that someone is you.

*A wee* bit of heaven

   drifted down from above—

A handful of happiness, a heart full of love.

The mystery of life so sacred and sweet,

The giver of joy so deep and complete.

Precious and priceless, so loveable, too—

The world's sweetest miracle, baby, is you.

$\mathcal{M}$any kind of trouble Dad reaches out his hand,

And you can always count on him

to help and understand. . .

And while we do not praise Dad

as often as we should,

We love him and admire him,

and while that's understood,

It's only fair to emphasize

his importance and his worth,

For if there were no loving dads,

this would be a loveless earth.

*Mothers* are special people
in a million different ways,
And merit loving compliments and many words of praise,
For a mother's aspiration is for her family's success,
To make the family proud of her
and bring them happiness. . .
And like our heavenly Father, she's a patient, loving guide,
Someone we can count on to be always on our side.

*There's* a road I call remembrance
where I walk each day with you.
It's a pleasant, happy road, my dear,
all filled with memories true.
Today it leads me through a spot
where I can dream awhile,
And in its tranquil peacefulness
I touch your hand and smile.

*With* faith in each other and faith in the Lord

May your marriage be blessed

   with love's priceless reward,

For love that endures and makes life worth living

Is built on strong faith and unselfish giving. . .

So have faith, and the Lord

   will guide both of you through

The glorious new life that is waiting for you.

*Love* in all its ecstasy is such a fragile thing,

Like gossamer in cloudless skies

    or a hummingbird's small wing. . .

But love that lasts forever

    must be made of something strong—

The kind of strength that's gathered

    when the heart can hear no song.

*Now* you're Mrs. instead of Miss,

And you've sealed your wedding vows with a kiss.

Your future lies in your hands, my dear,

For it's yours to mold from year to year.

God grant that you make it a beautiful thing,

With all of the blessings that marriage can bring.

*I come* to meet You, God,

   and as I linger here

I seem to feel You very near.

A rustling leaf, a rolling slope

Speak to my heart of endless hope.

The sun just rising in the sky,

The waking birdlings as they fly,

The grass all wet with morning dew

Are telling me I just met You.

*Once* again I've met You, God,

And worshipped on Your holy sod. . .

For who could see the dawn break through

Without a glimpse of heaven and You?

For who but God could make the day

And softly put the night away?

*Sometimes* when faith is running low

And I cannot fathom why things are so,

I walk among the flowers that grow

And learn the answers to all I would know. . .

For among my flowers I have come to see

Life's miracle and its mystery,

And standing in silence and reverie,

My faith comes flooding back to me.

*Oh,* give us faith to believe again

That peace on earth, goodwill to men

Will follow this winter of man's mind

And awaken his heart and make him kind. . .

And just as great nature sends the spring

To give new birth to each sleeping thing,

God, grant rebirth to man's slumbering soul

And help him forsake his selfish goal.

*God* lives in the beauty that comes with spring—

The colorful flower, the birds that sing—

And He lives in people as kind as you,

And He lives in all the nice things you do.

# Index

197, 199, 200, 206, 220, 242, 244, 248, 257, 258, 260, 264, 266, 267, 271, 281, 286, 290, 301, 318, 325, 331, 332

*Easter:* 15, 48, 58, 61, 106, 124, 125, 166, 298, 301, 303, 311

*Eternity:* 8, 11, 12, 15, 18, 19, 30, 35, 44, 61, 81, 102, 115, 118, 122, 125, 126, 128, 138, 140, 164, 166, 171, 258, 301, 311

*Faith:* 14, 15, 27, 40, 49, 56, 59, 63, 72, 78, 86, 91, 98, 105, 120, 122, 134, 153, 156, 173, 175, 189, 194, 197, 199, 201, 203, 204, 206, 209, 211, 219, 242, 249, 252, 259, 260, 267, 268, 271, 272, 273, 274, 275, 276, 282, 283, 284, 285, 286, 290, 300, 303, 304, 306, 307, 309, 338, 343

*Family:* 9, 129, 132, 140, 158, 280, 315, 334, 335, 336

*Fatherhood:* 315, 335

*Friendship:* 25, 29, 46, 47, 51, 52, 55, 57, 65, 84, 89, 95, 97, 106, 108, 109, 119, 121, 138, 157, 185, 202, 213, 217, 223, 228, 229, 230, 233, 234, 236, 237, 239, 240, 241, 243, 255, 292, 295, 305, 329, 331, 332, 333, 337, 345

*God's love:* 12, 13, 14, 22, 24, 31, 47, 50, 59, 75, 76, 77, 78, 82, 85, 90, 92, 97, 100, 104, 110, 114, 116, 117, 119, 144, 146, 149, 154, 156, 159, 160, 161, 163, 174, 176, 177, 178, 181, 183, 184, 186, 187, 189, 191, 192, 194, 195, 196, 197, 199, 203, 204, 206, 209, 210, 211, 213, 216, 217, 219, 220, 221, 223, 224, 226, 230, 232, 233, 237, 242, 243, 244, 245, 247, 248, 251, 252, 256, 257, 264, 267, 271, 273, 275, 278, 279, 281, 287, 288, 301, 306, 310, 313, 316, 318, 323, 325, 328, 332, 336

| *God's power:* | 32, 38, 62, 83, 101, 104, 110, 117, 145, 153, 244, 257 |
|---|---|

| *Grace:* | 13, 40, 92, 94, 102, 115, 124, 169, 178, 191, 192, 196, 201, 210, 238, 256, 290, 300, 306, 310, 311, 316, 317 |
|---|---|

| *Hope:* | 8, 11, 13, 17, 19, 21, 22, 30, 41, 43, 62, 66, 80, 83, 85, 94, 99, 103, 118, 122, 131, 133, 136, 139, 180, 191, 193, 198, 199, 200, 201, 226, 229, 235, 245, 246, 248, 250, 251, 254, 255, 257, 258, 259, 260, 262, 265, 269, 270, 279, 302, 309, 321, 325 |
|---|---|

| *Joy:* | 7, 20, 21, 42, 57, 65, 70, 84, 85, 97, 102, 115, 129, 133, 136, 139, 154, 155, 176, 180, 185, 202, 212, 226, 230, 234, 237, 247, 268, 269, 270, 288, 302, 321 |
|---|---|

| | |
|---|---|
| *Love:* | 37, 57, 60, 89, 121, 132, 134, 143, 158, 168, 213, 214, 216, 230, 237, 254, 255, 280, 284, 295, 309, 312, 313, 314, 319, 320, 322, 323, 324, 326, 328, 330, 334, 335, 336, 339 |
| *Marriage:* | 96, 141, 216, 323, 330, 338, 339, 340 |
| *Motherhood:* | 9, 140, 158, 336 |
| *Nature:* | 7, 26, 28, 32, 38, 42, 44, 46, 58, 61, 64, 68, 78, 85, 86, 106, 107, 109, 110, 118, 145, 147, 166, 217, 221, 222, 244, 266, 281, 298, 302, 329, 341, 342, 343, 344, 345 |
| *Peace:* | 16, 20, 26, 28, 48, 67, 90, 101, 116, 142, 146, 147, 148, 170, 181, 183, 187, 188, 190, 207, 220, 240, 244, 263, 266, 269, 270, 281, 284, 307, 318, 320, 337 |

| *Perseverance:* | 17, 21, 22, 24, 28, 31, 40, 41, 43, 62, 63, 72, 91, 98, 112, 113, 117, 120, 153, 154, 175, 179, 189, 197, 198, 202, 205, 235, 245, 246, 248, 249, 250, 251, 252, 253, 254, 259, 260, 264, 265, 266, 267, 268, 271, 272, 274, 275, 277, 278, 279, 282, 283, 285, 286, 321, 325 |
|---|---|
| *Praise:* | 7, 72, 137, 155, 222, 247 |
| *Prayer:* | 9, 10, 12, 16, 20, 25, 27, 34, 36, 48, 49, 50, 59, 66, 67, 68, 71, 73, 75, 84, 88, 90, 100, 101, 103, 123, 130, 131, 133, 134, 135, 136, 137, 142, 145, 146, 148, 150, 151, 152, 155, 156, 157, 159, 160, 161, 163, 164, 165, 167, 169, 170, 171, 172, 173, 175, 176, 177, 179, 180, 182, 183, 184, 188, 190, 191, 193, 194, 195, 200, 201, 207, 208, 215, 238, 272, 276, 292, 296, 303, 307, 308, 315, 323, 341, 342 |
| *Romance:* | 74, 95, 96, 141, 314, 324, 326, 327, 330, 339 |

*Sympathy:*    8, 19, 35, 102, 115, 118, 244, 258, 266, 331

*Thankfulness:*    7, 36, 52, 64, 76, 88, 113, 155, 195, 212, 240, 291, 292, 293, 294, 296, 297